Sacred Geometry: Mandalas

An Adult Coloring Book

An eclectic collection of sacred geometry inspired mandalas that will allow your imagination to create a virtual cornucopia of contemplative colors.

Dedicated to the love of my life - my soulmate Rebecca.

by Joseph Leon

Introduction

Coloring for adults is not as uncommon as some may believe. Doctors have known about the benefits since the early 1900s. Psychiatrist Carl Jung, the founder of analytical psychology, prescribed coloring to his patients to calm and center their minds. He did this using mandalas: circular designs with concentric shapes similar to the Gothic churches' rose windows. Doctors today continue to follow Jung's recommendation to help lower anxiety, stabilize mood, improve memory, increase attention span, exercise fine motor skills, training the brain to focus and even serve as a sleep aid. It has also proven helpful to those dealing with depression, dementia and PTSD.

Like meditation, coloring also allows us to switch off our brains from other thoughts and focus only on the moment.

Get your coloring pencils or crayons ready and enjoy coloring this great collection of Sacred Geometry: Mandalas.

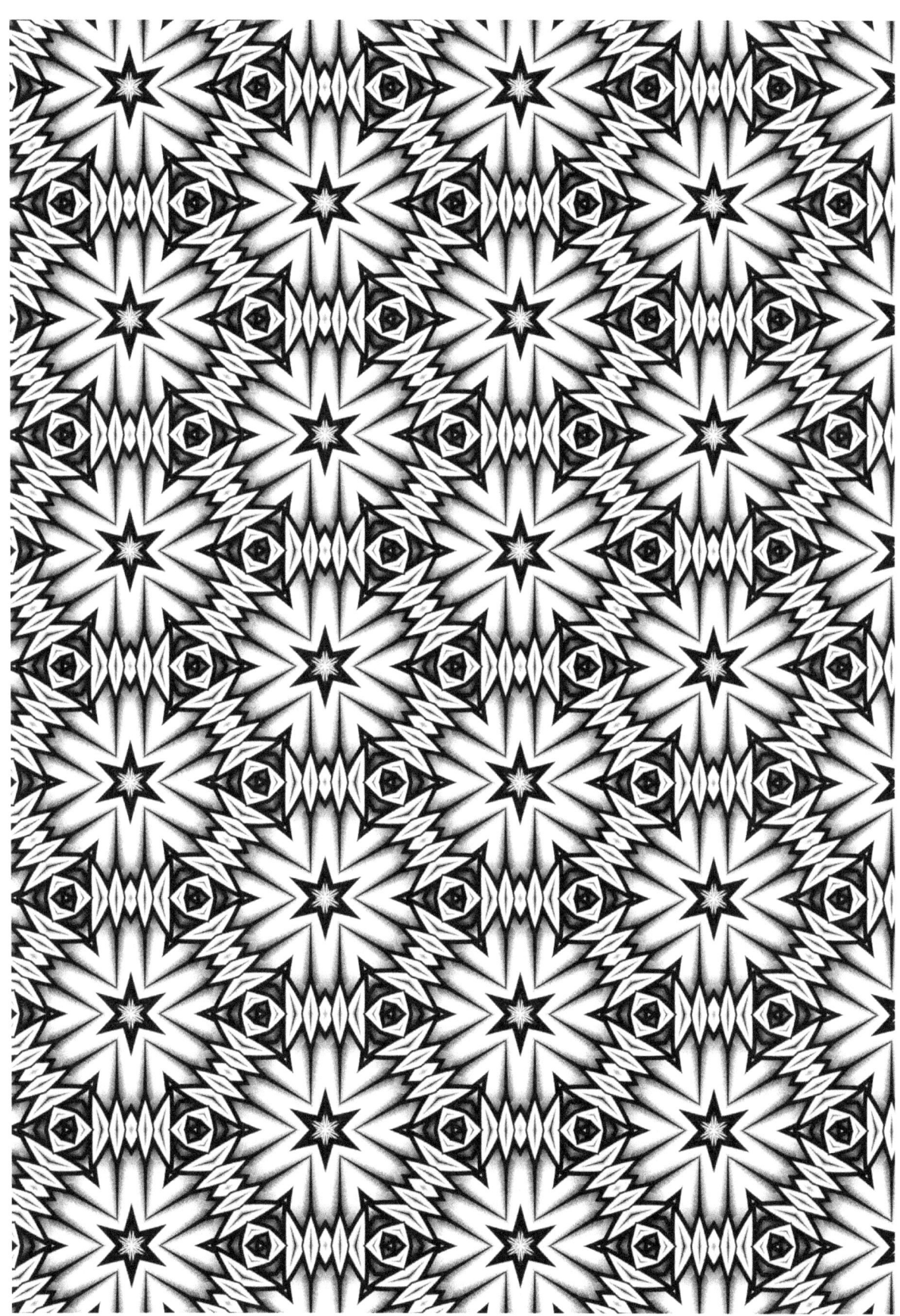

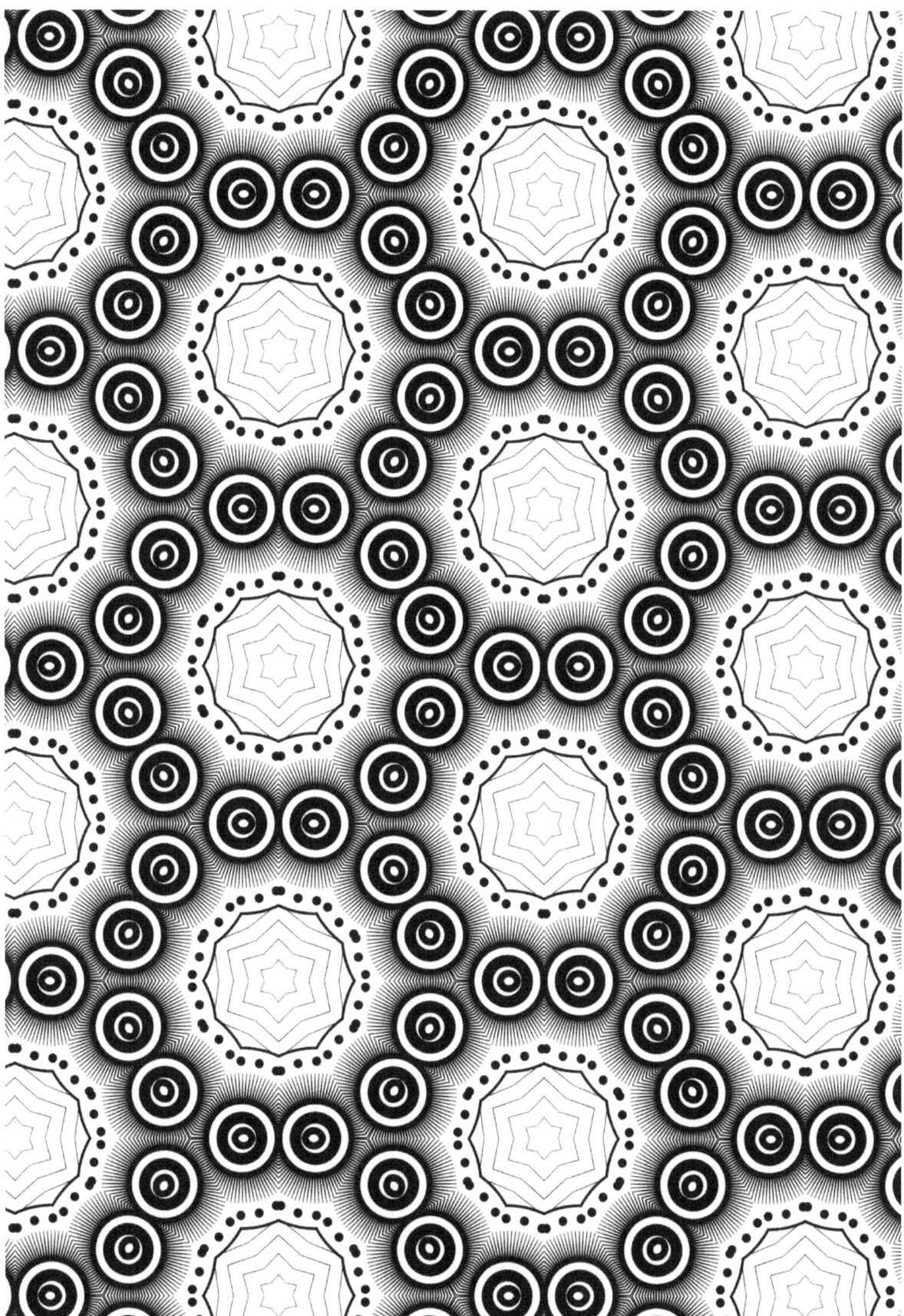

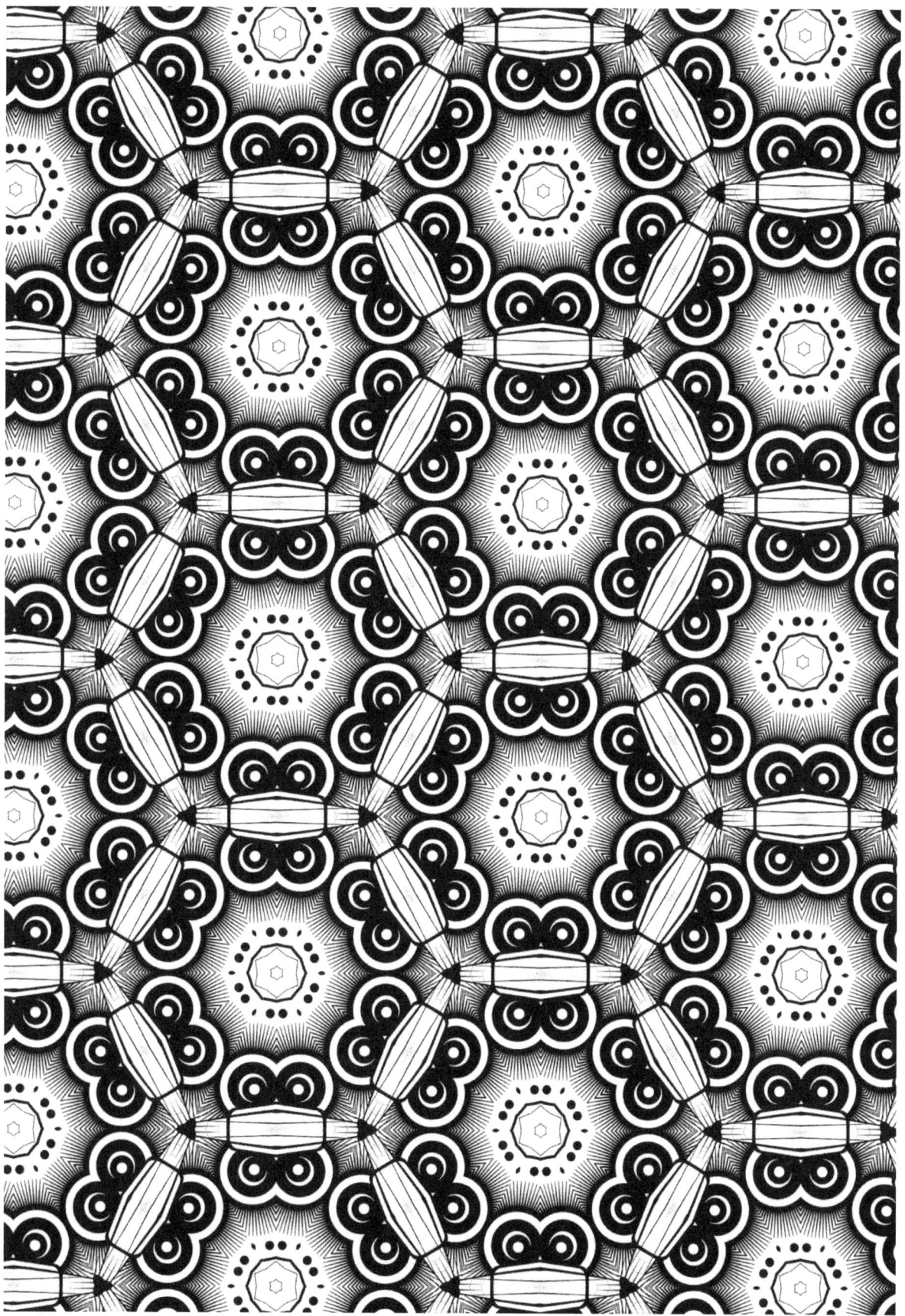

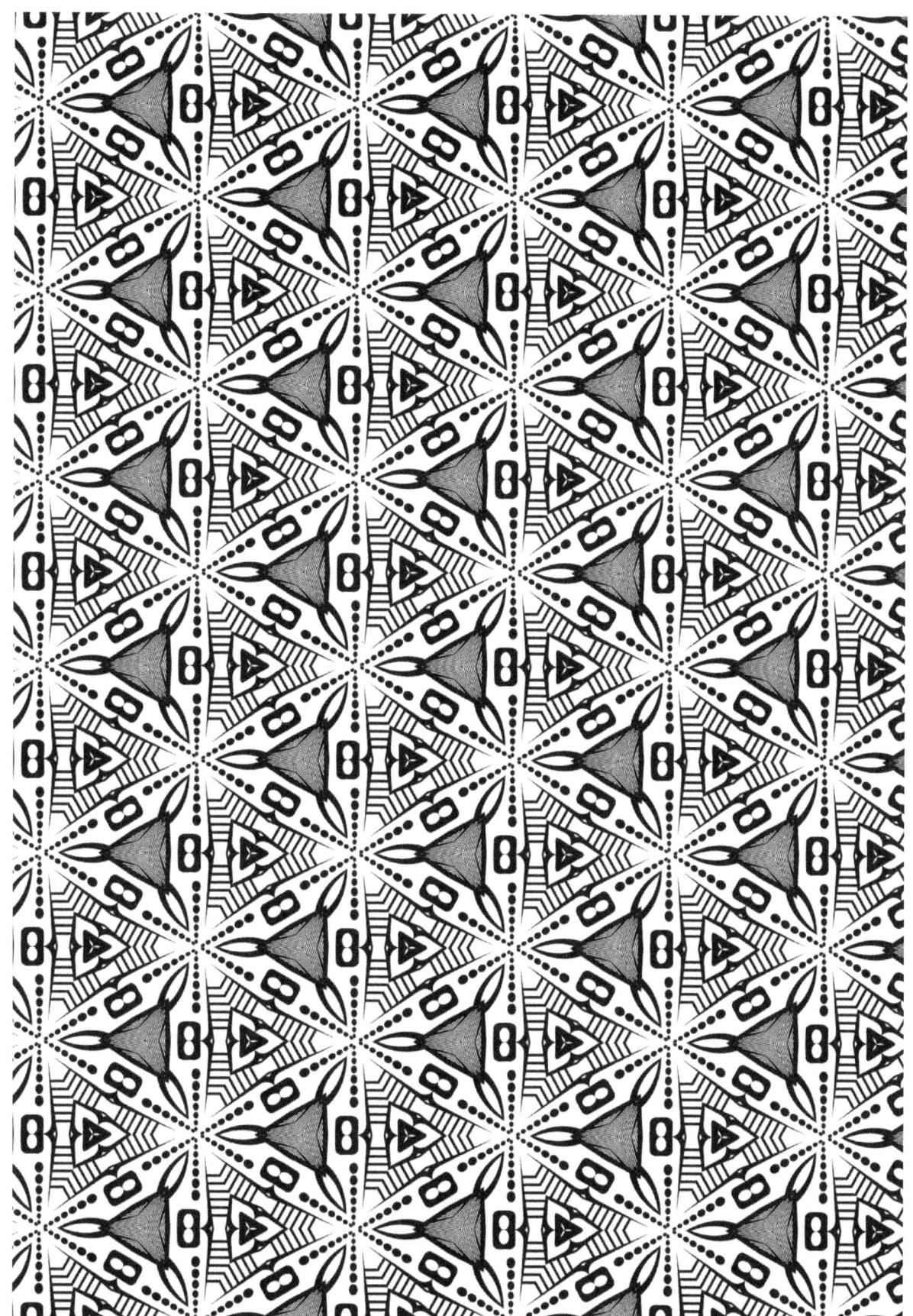

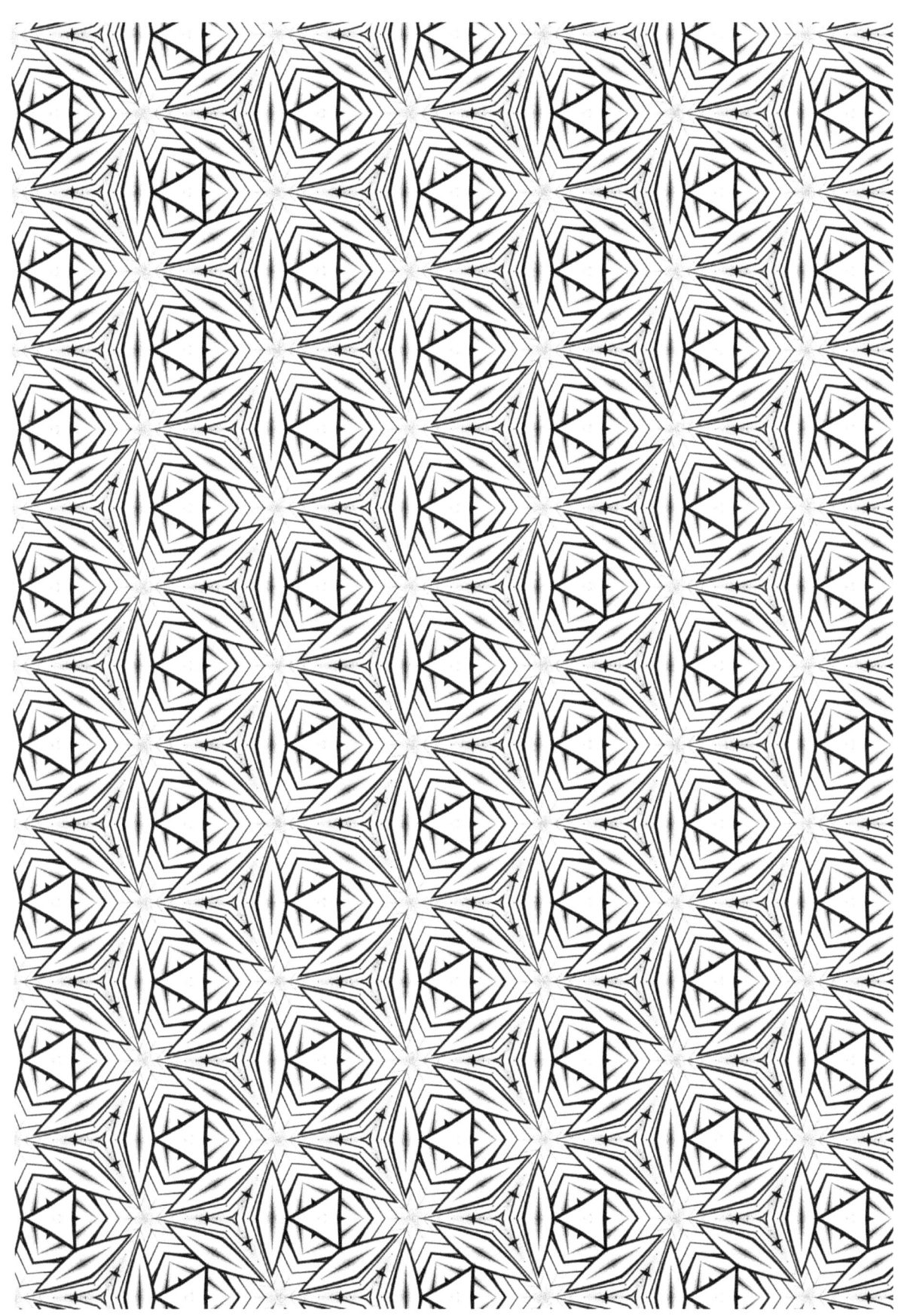

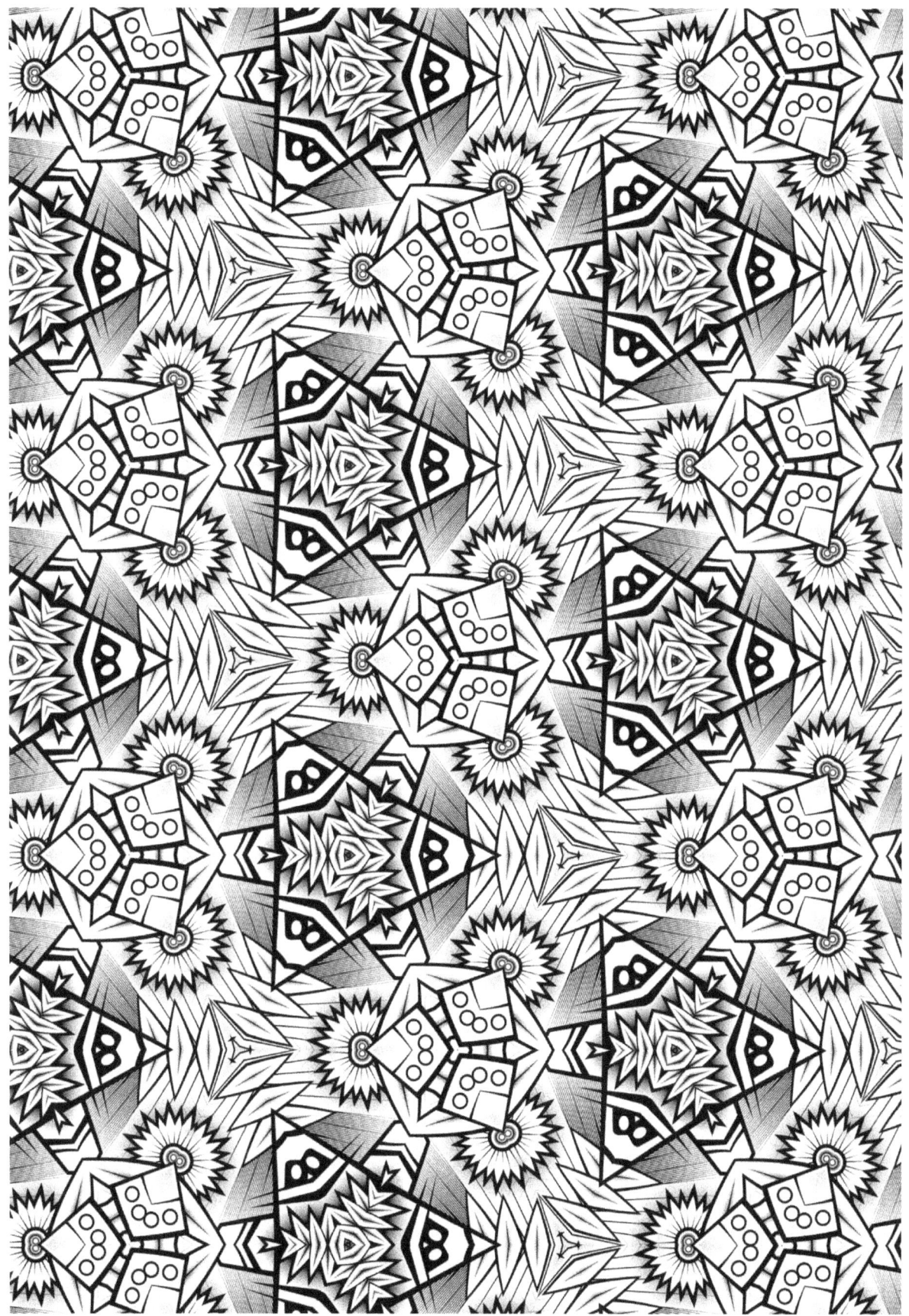

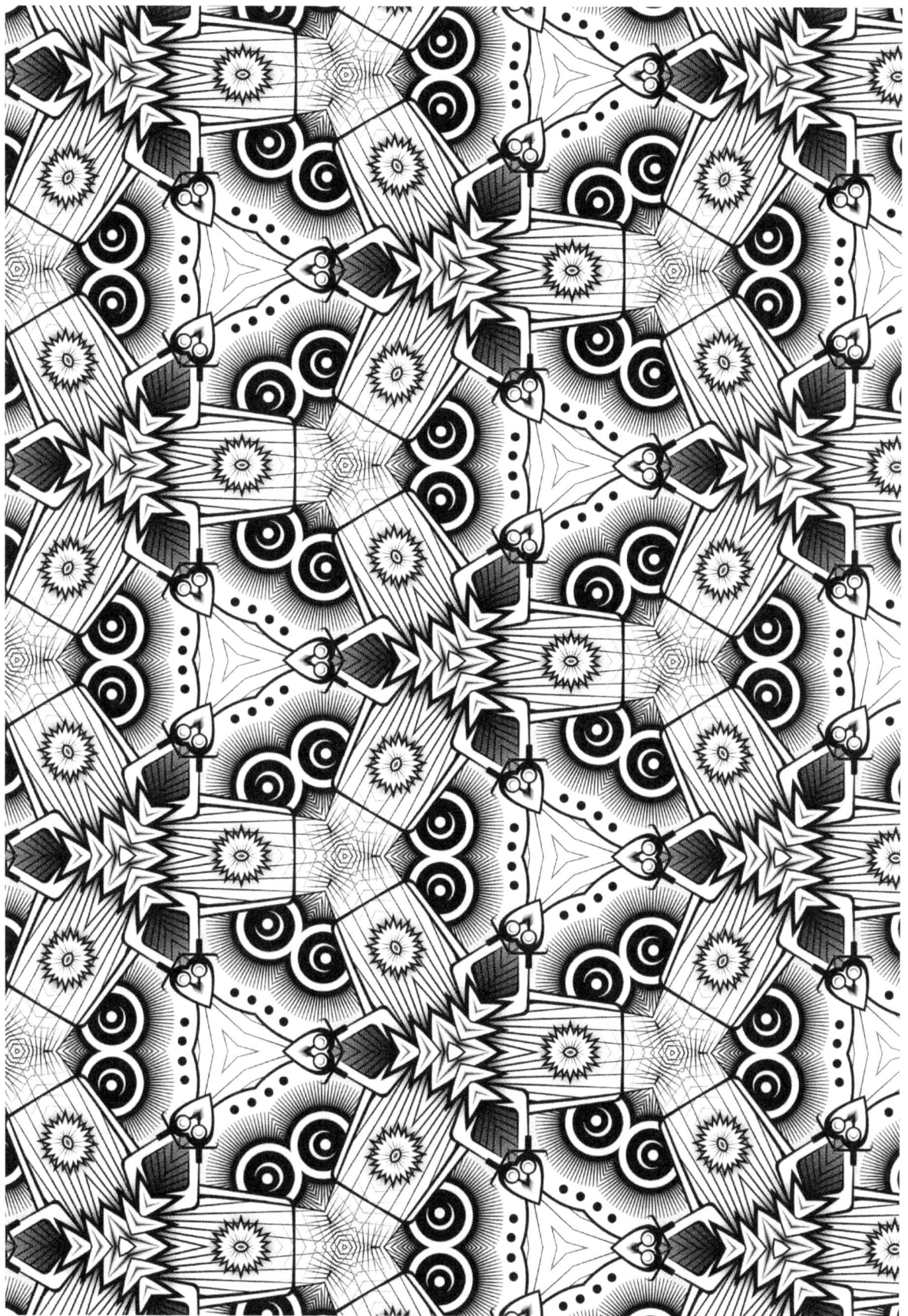

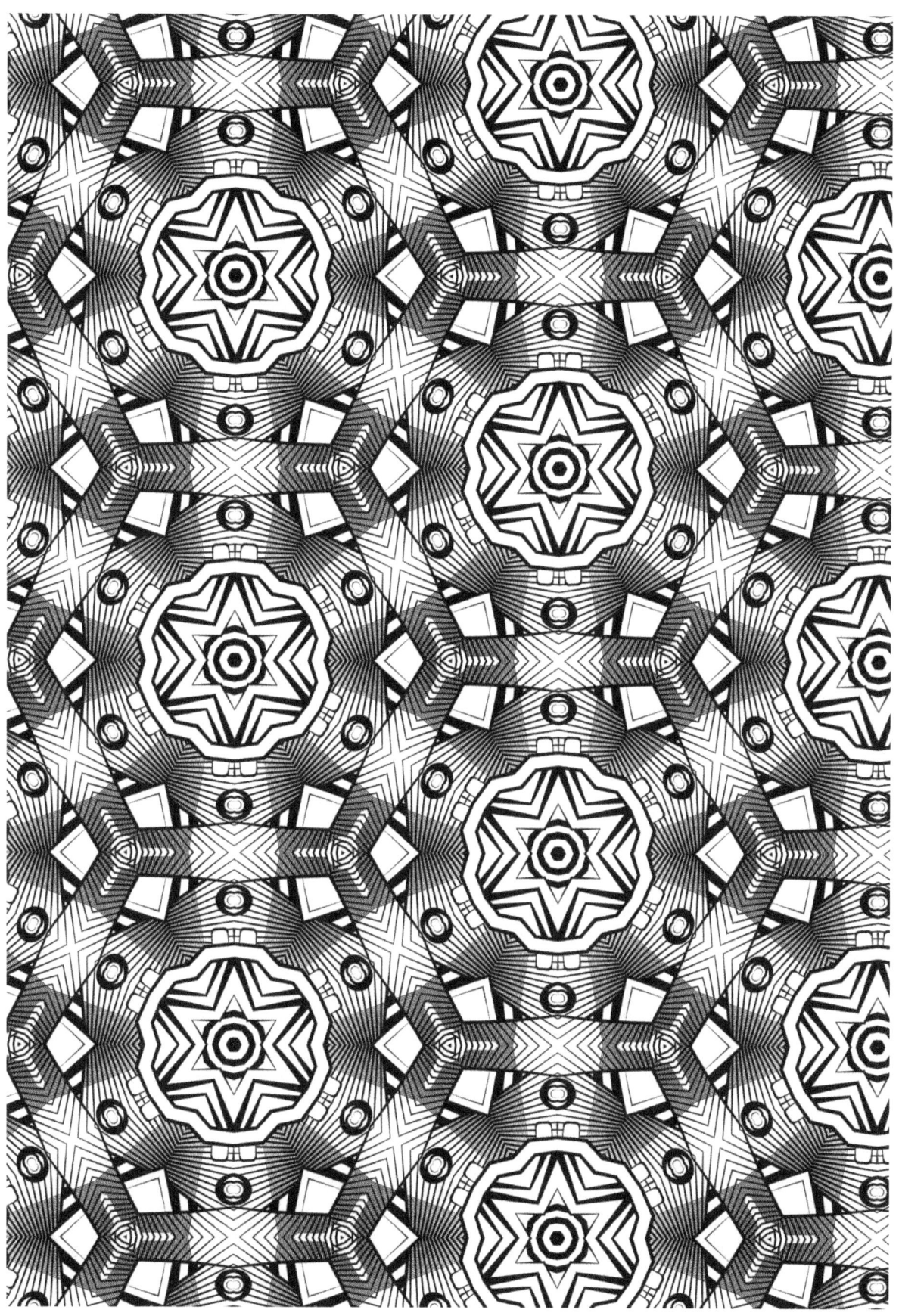

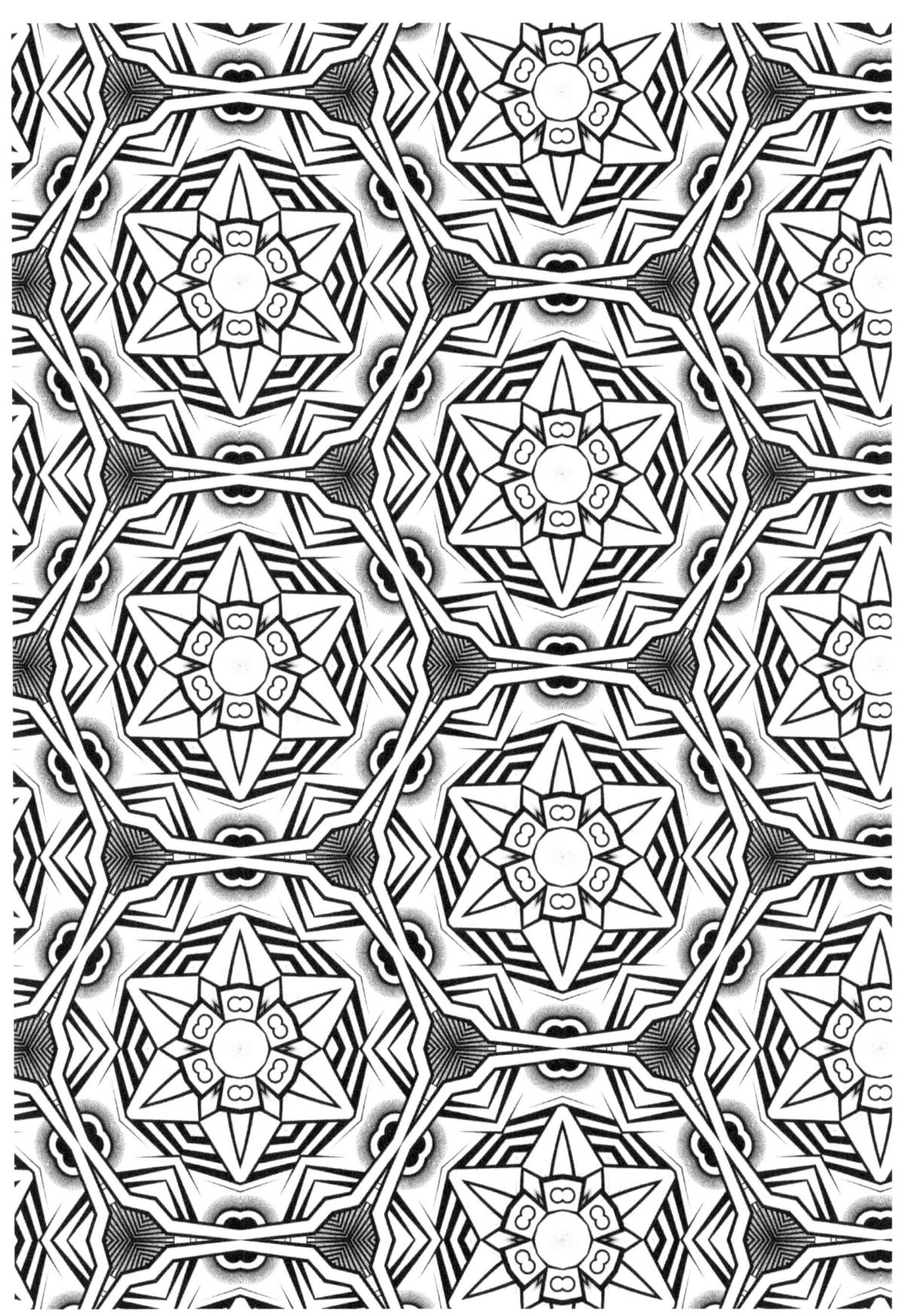

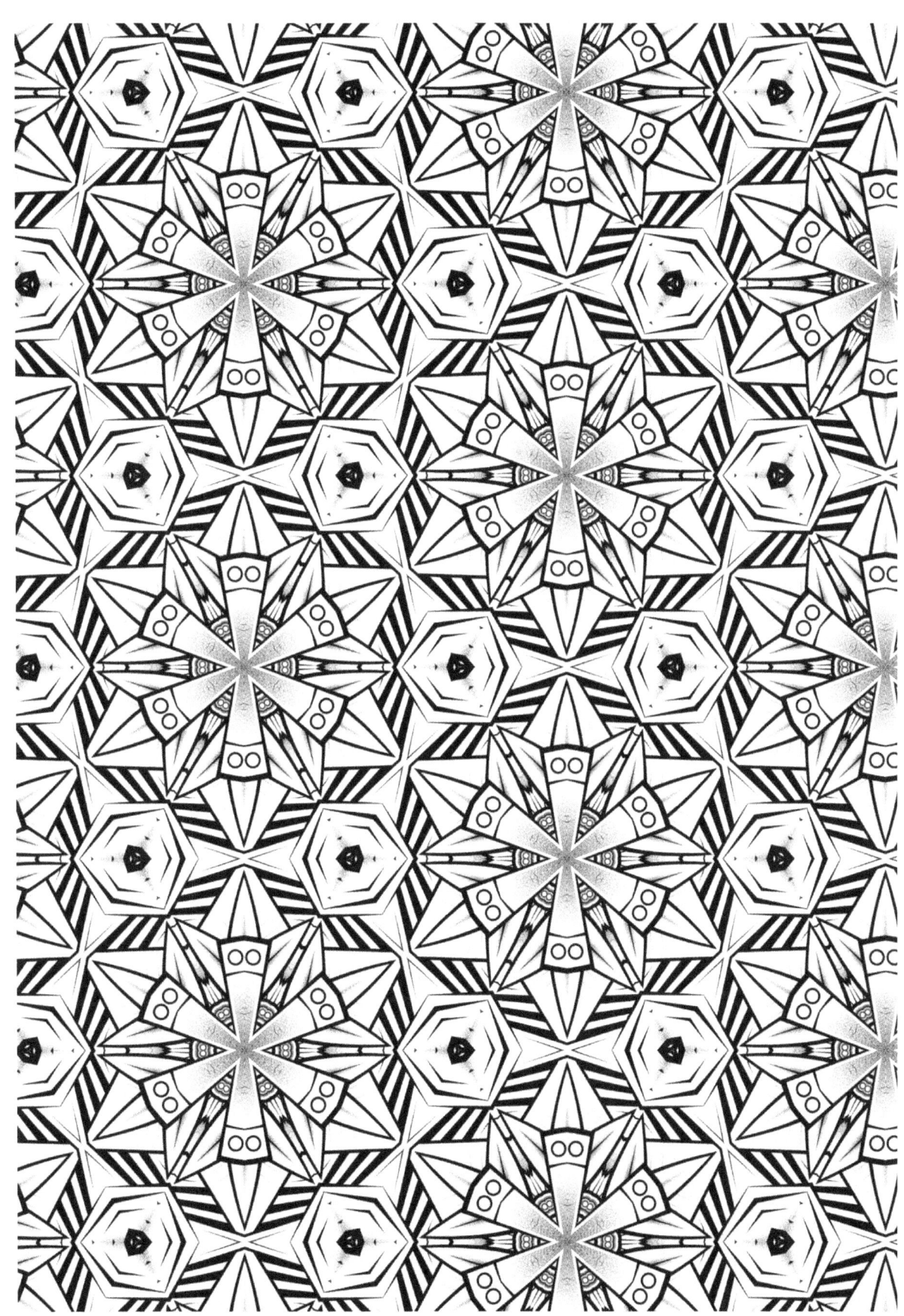

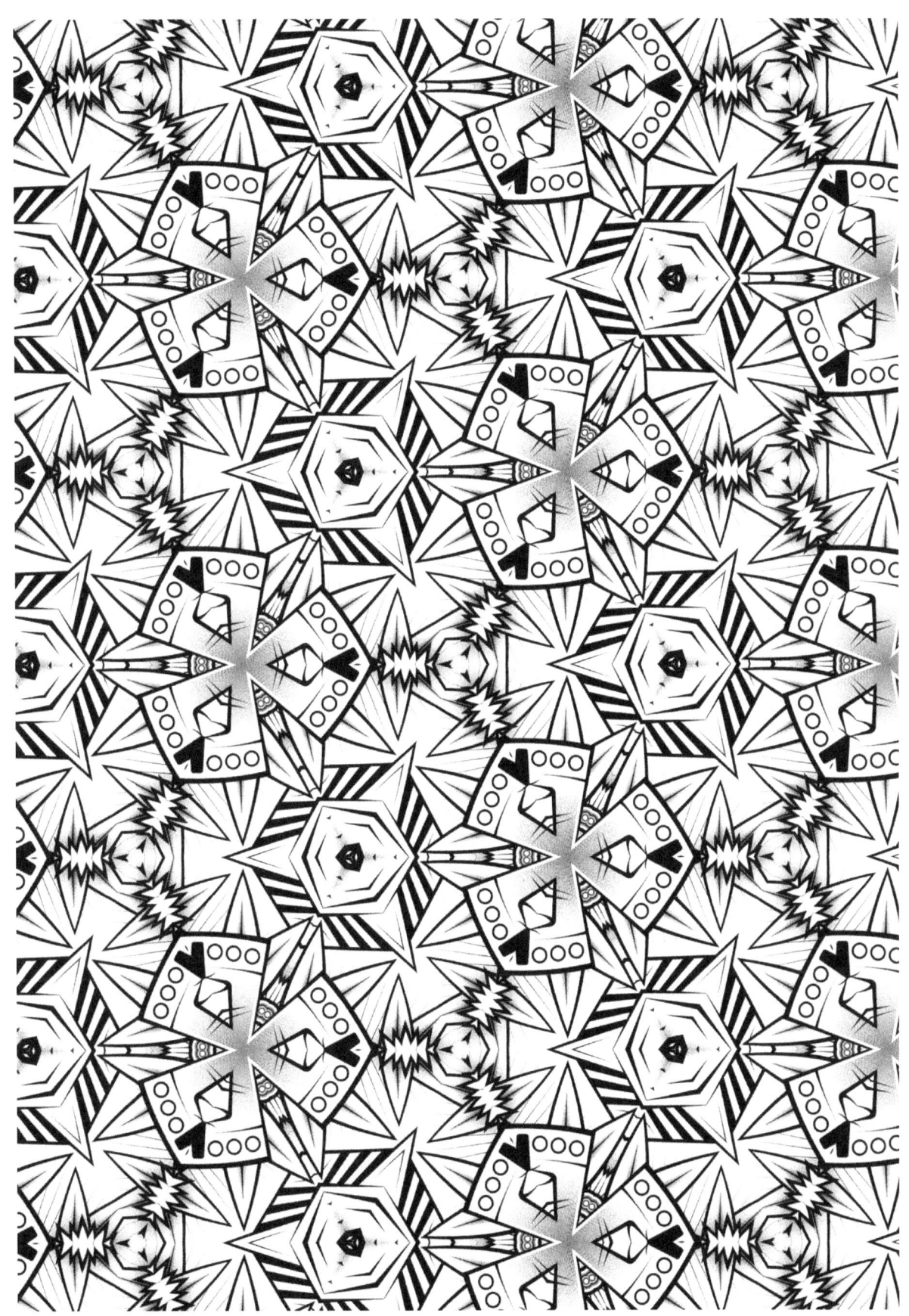

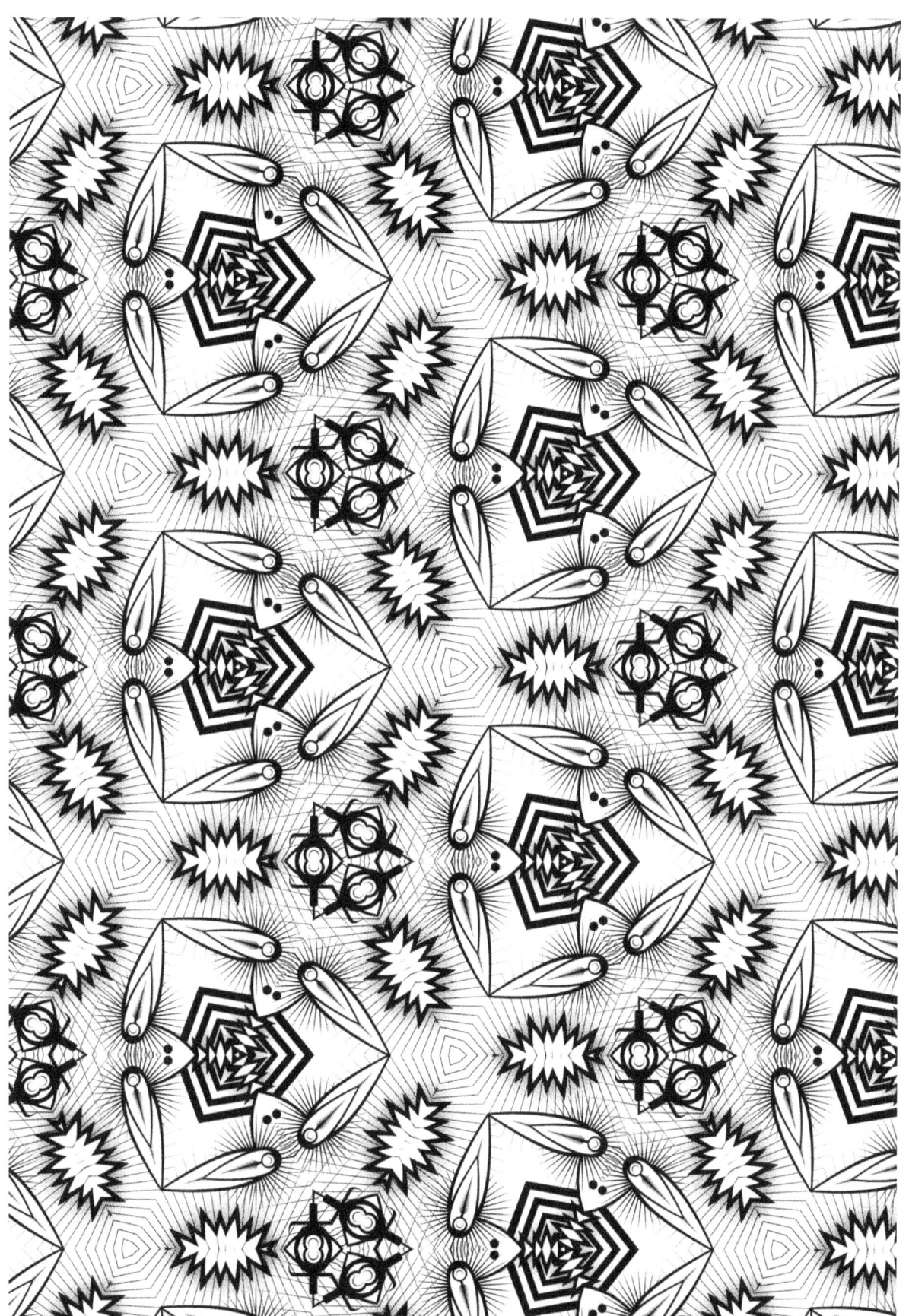

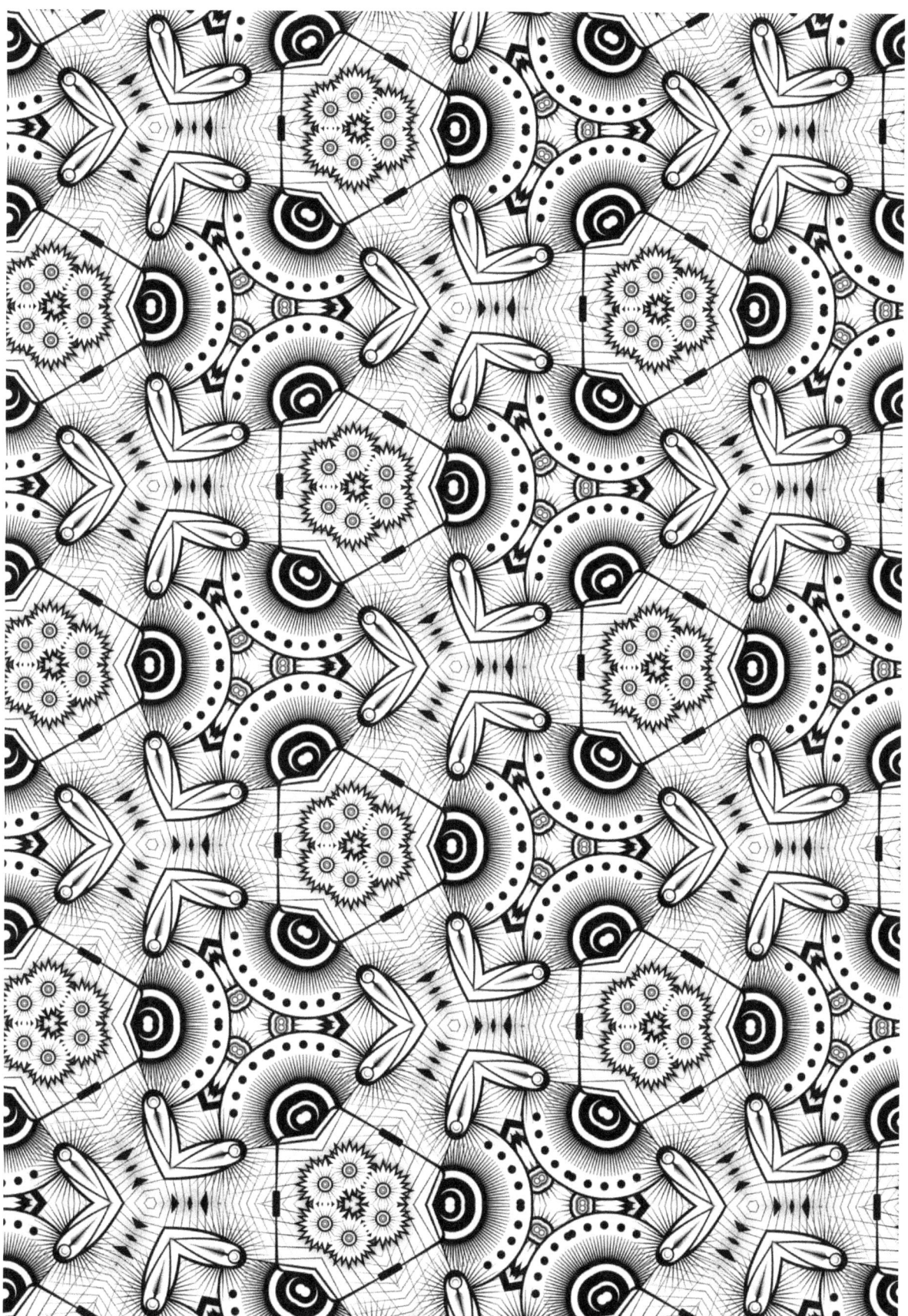

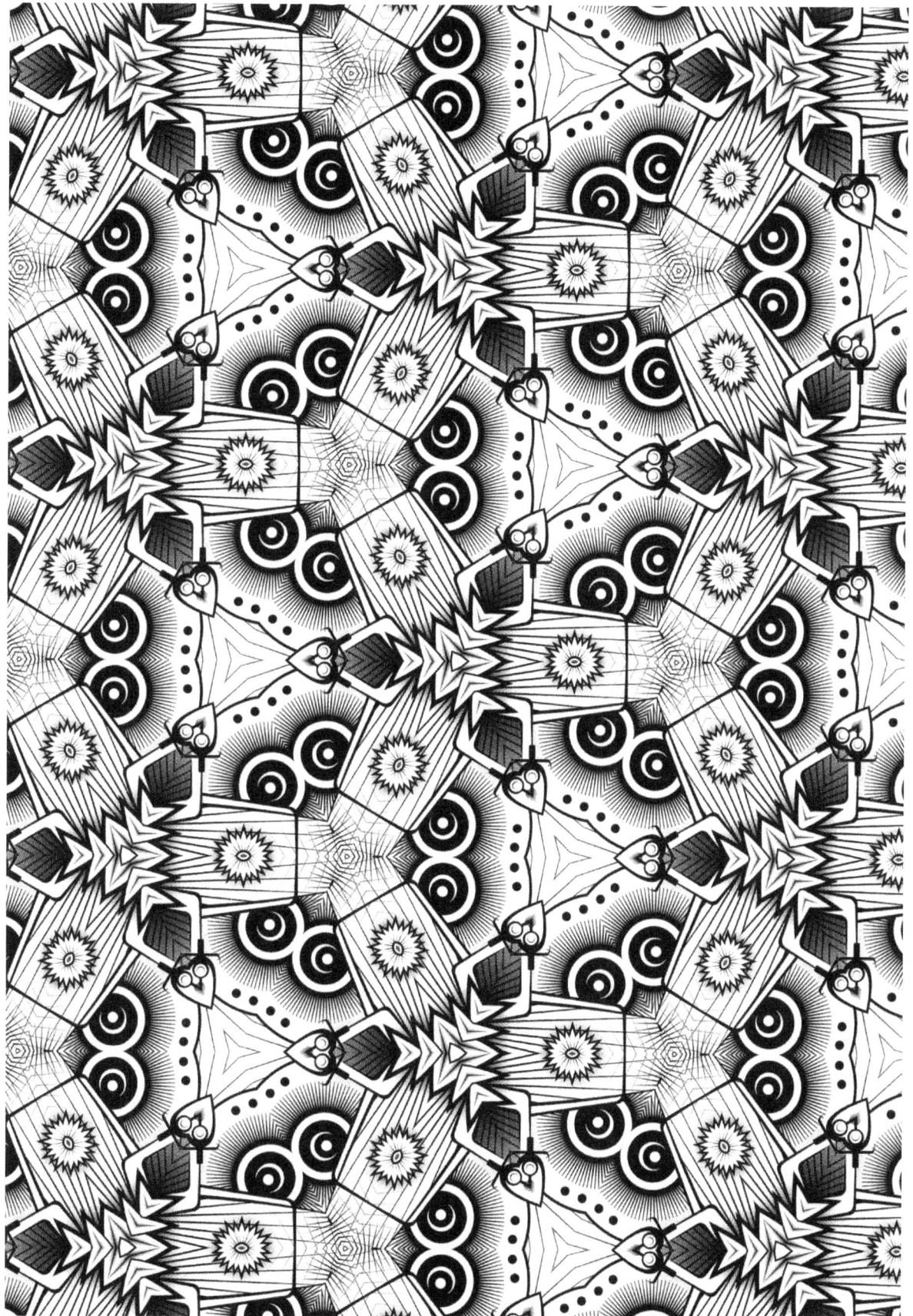

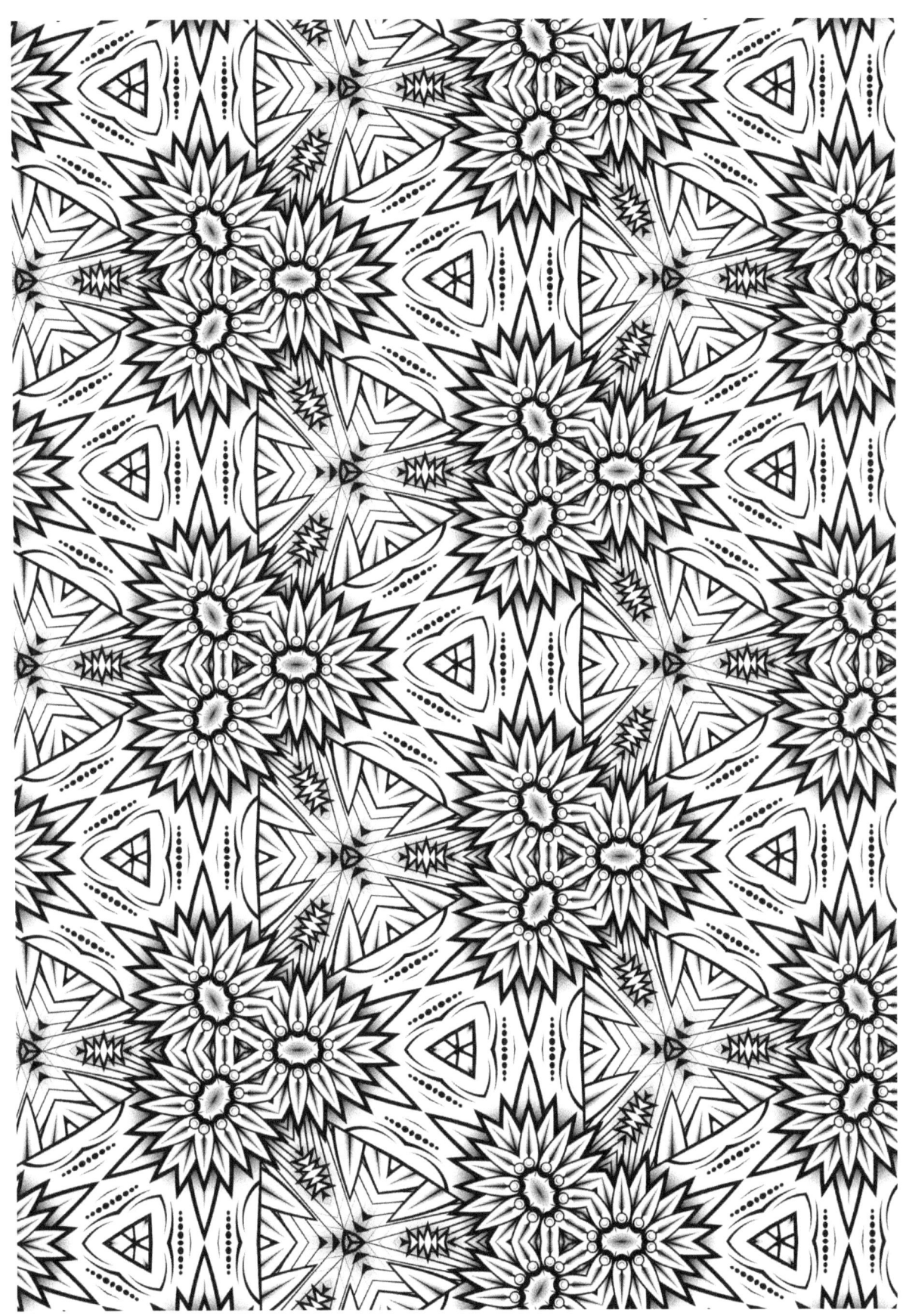

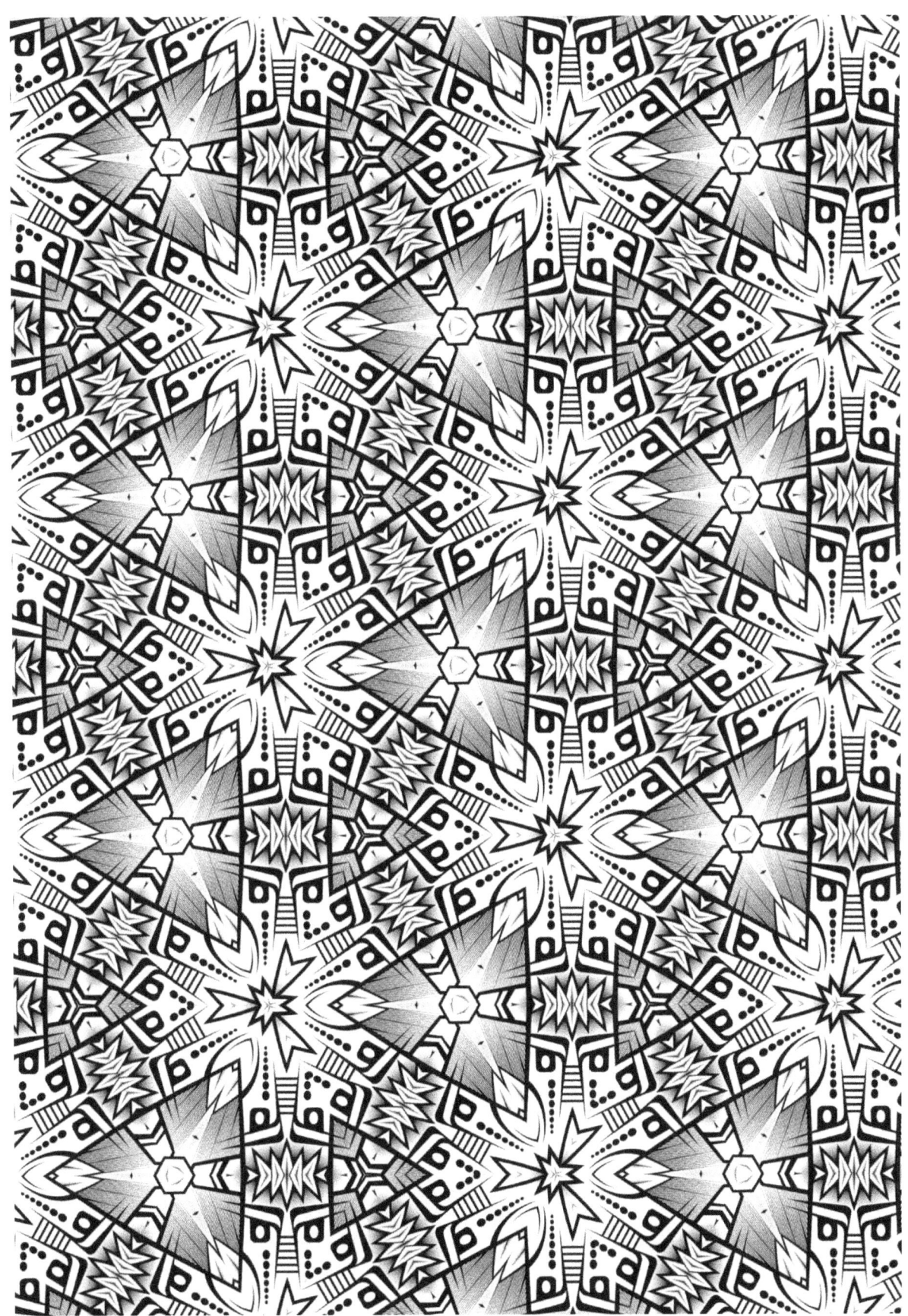

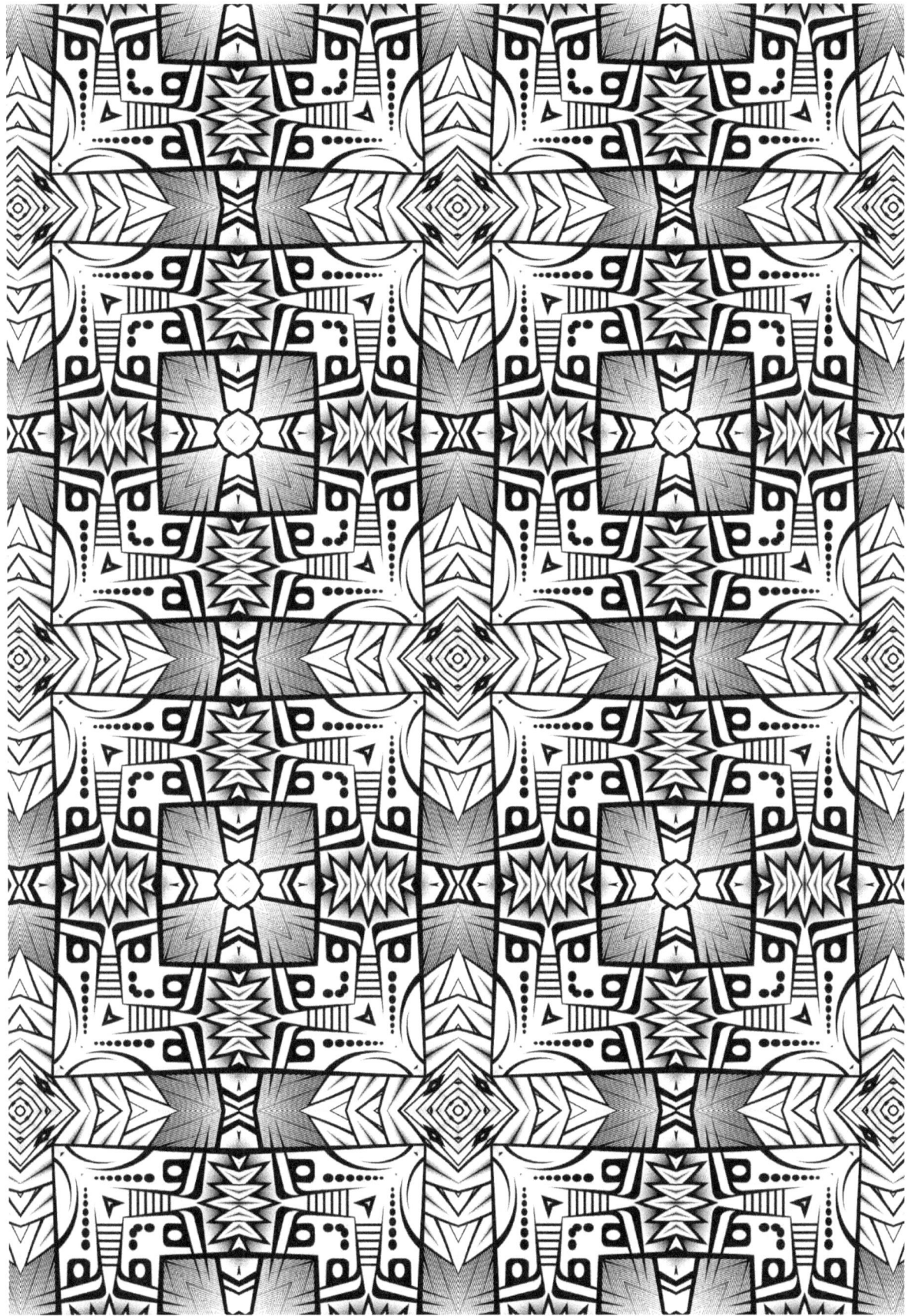

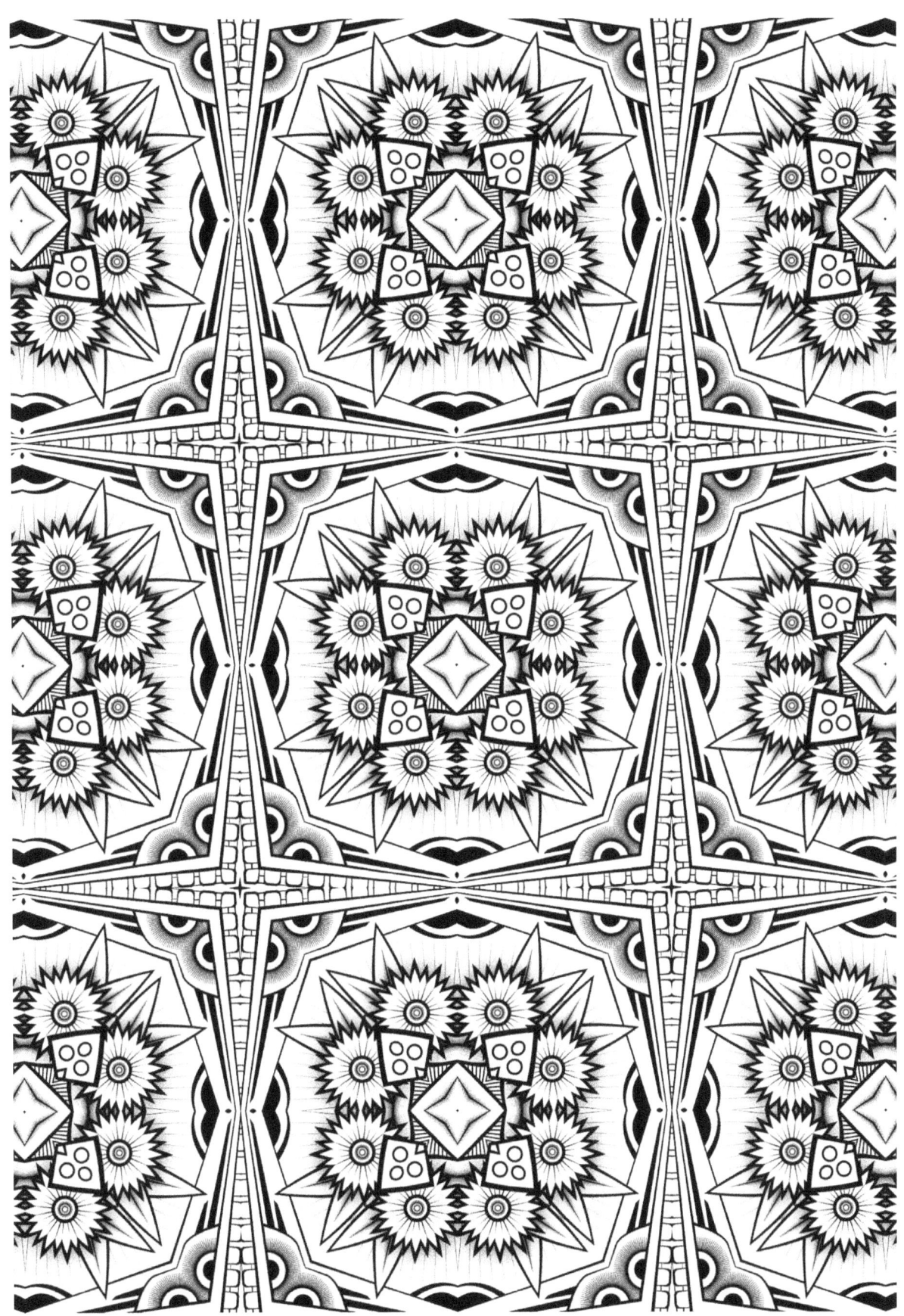

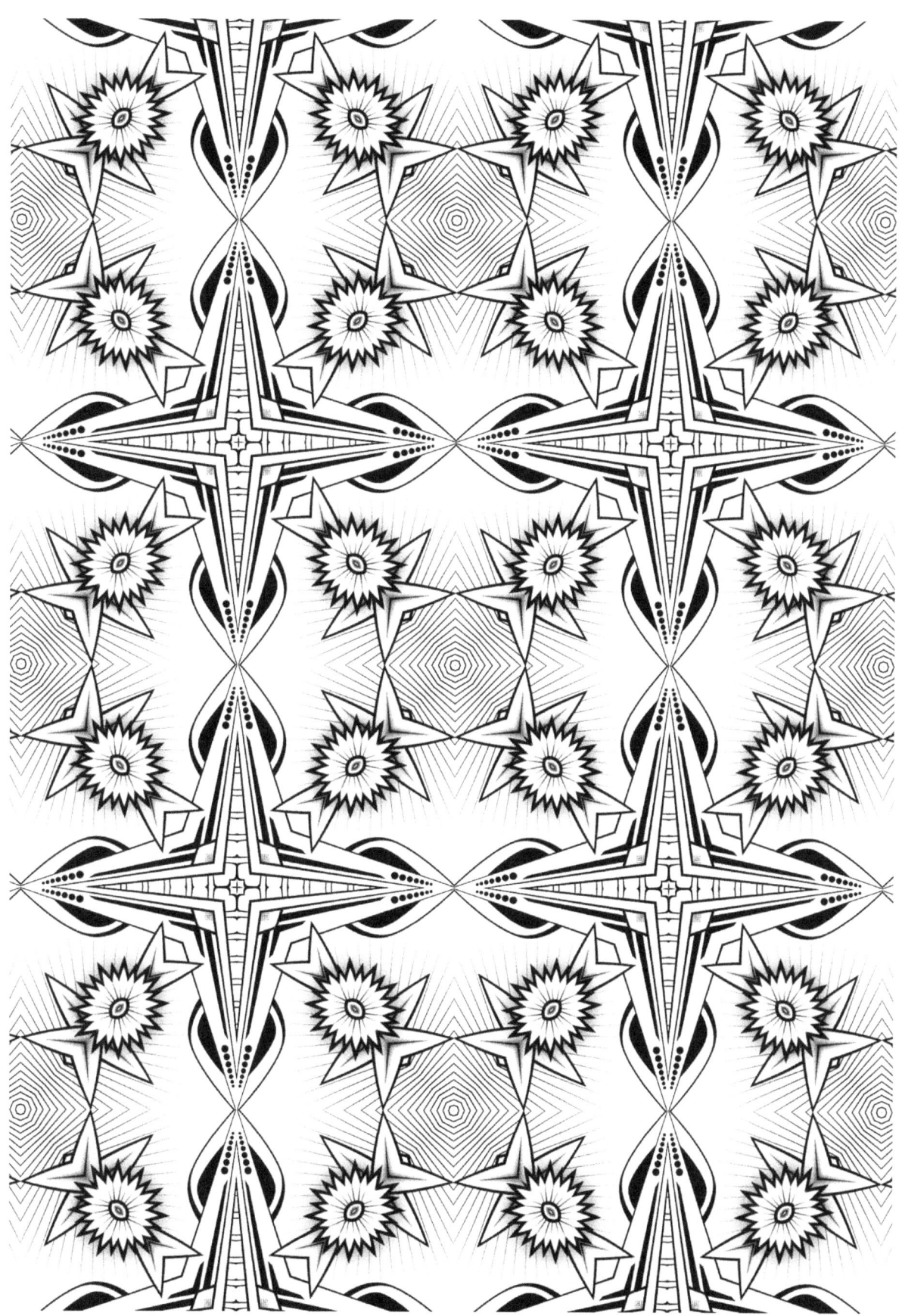

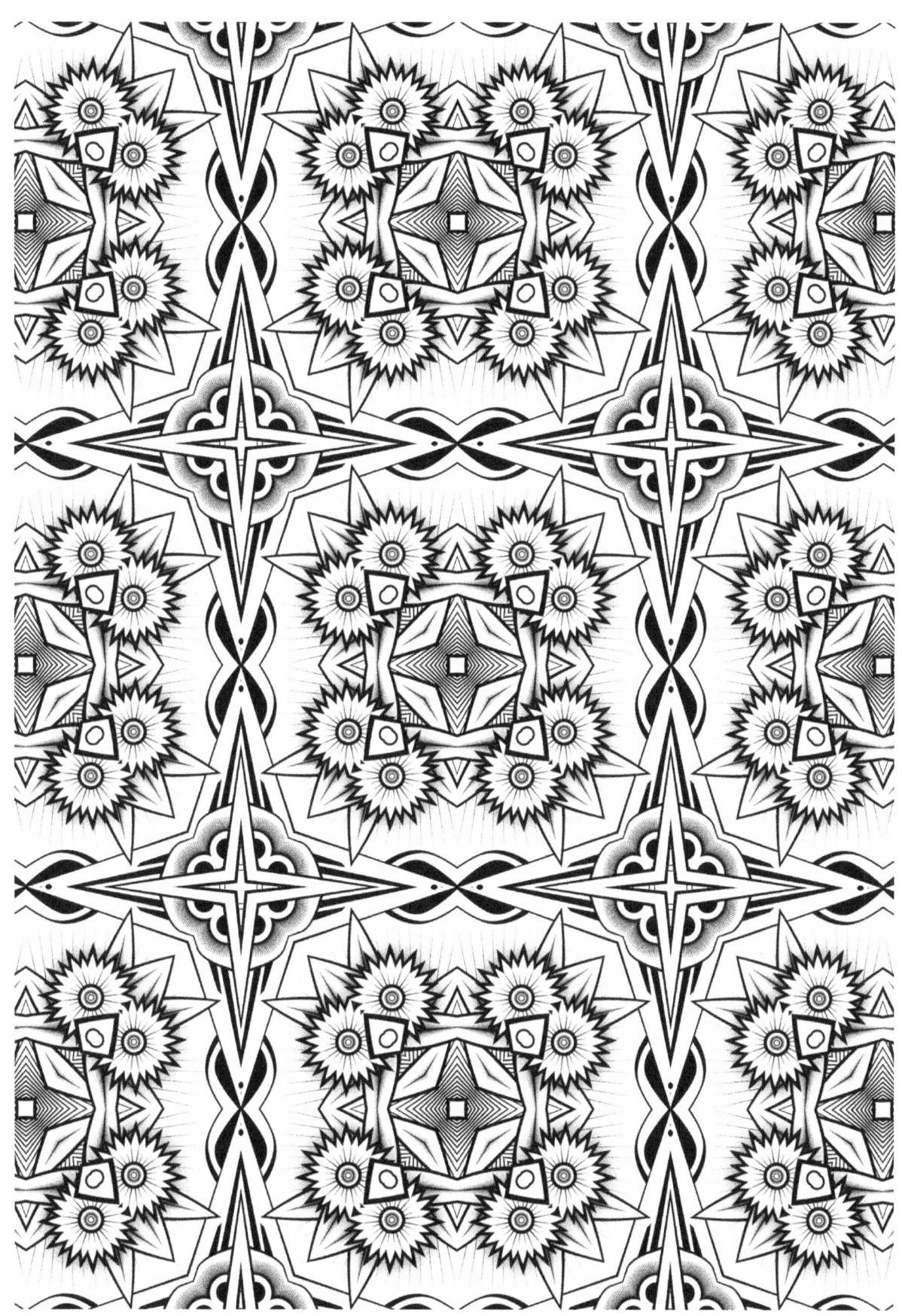

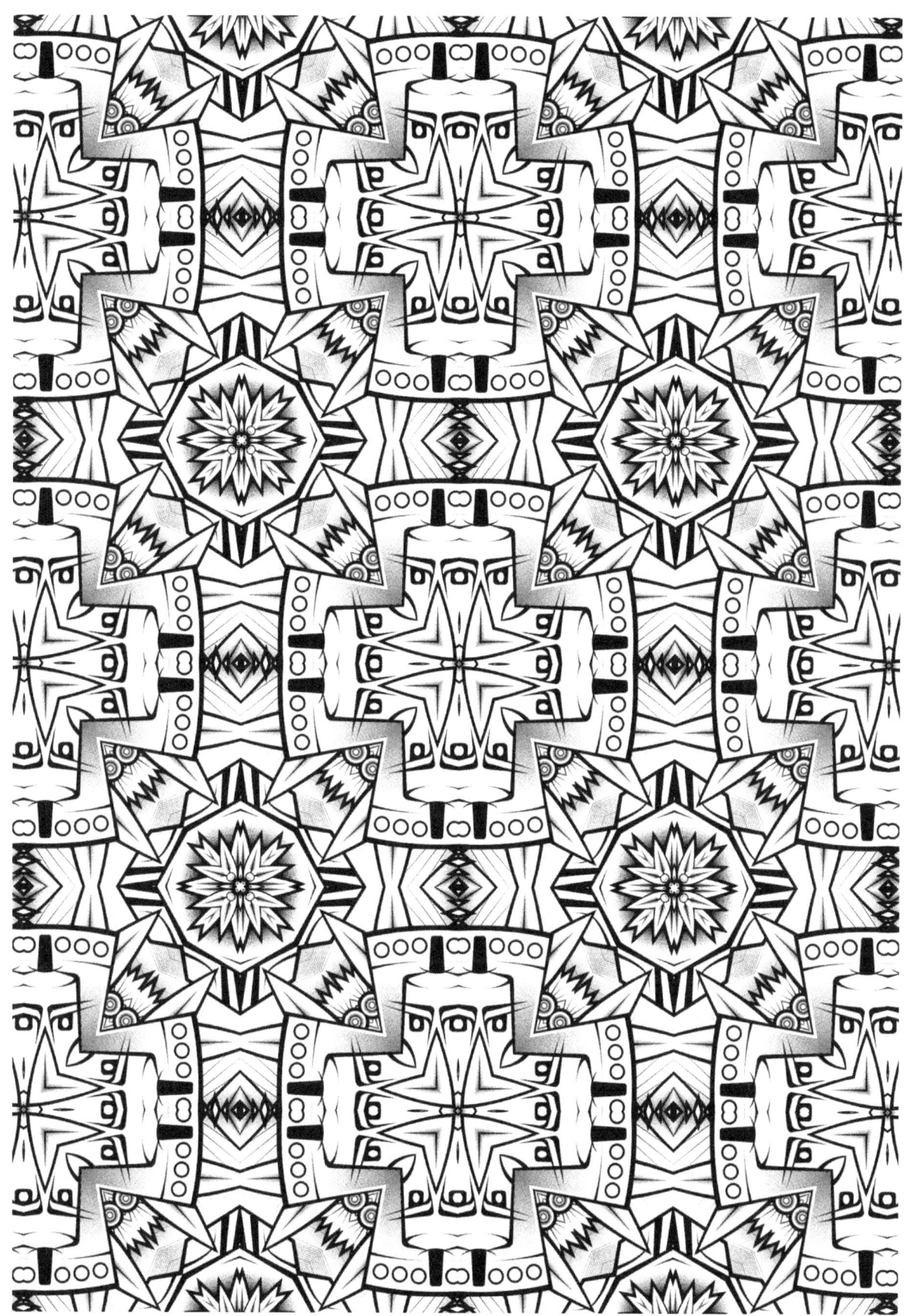

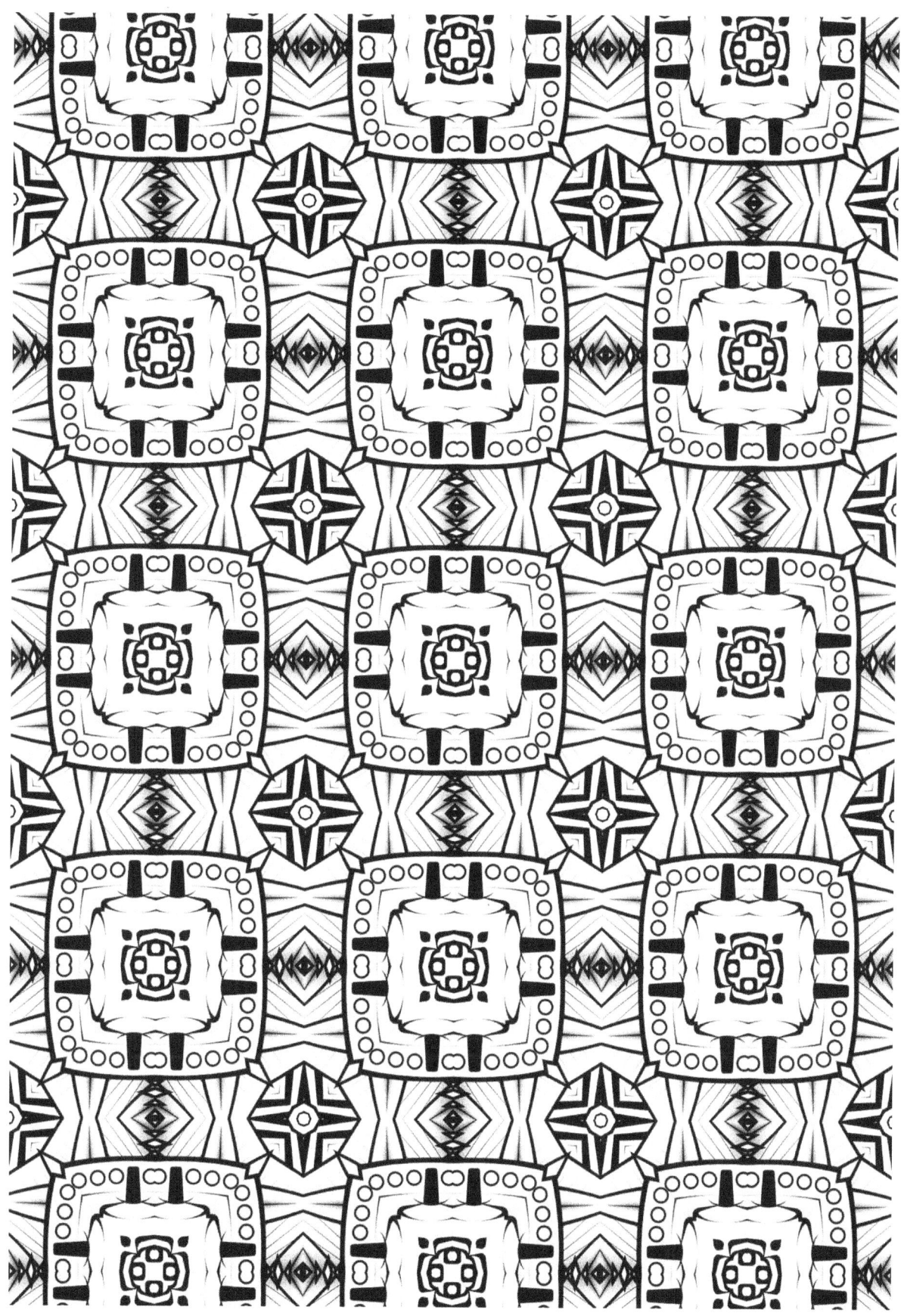

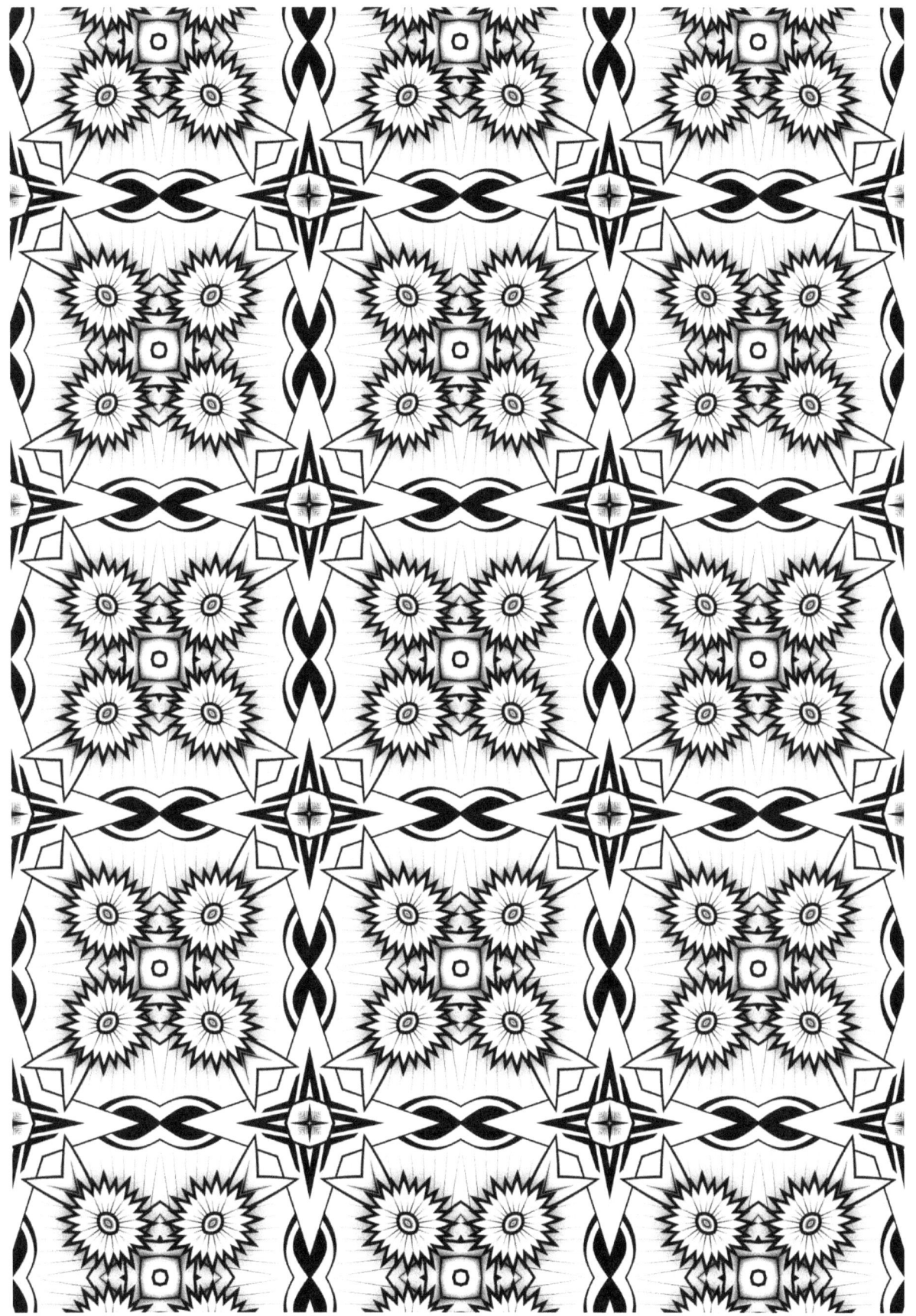

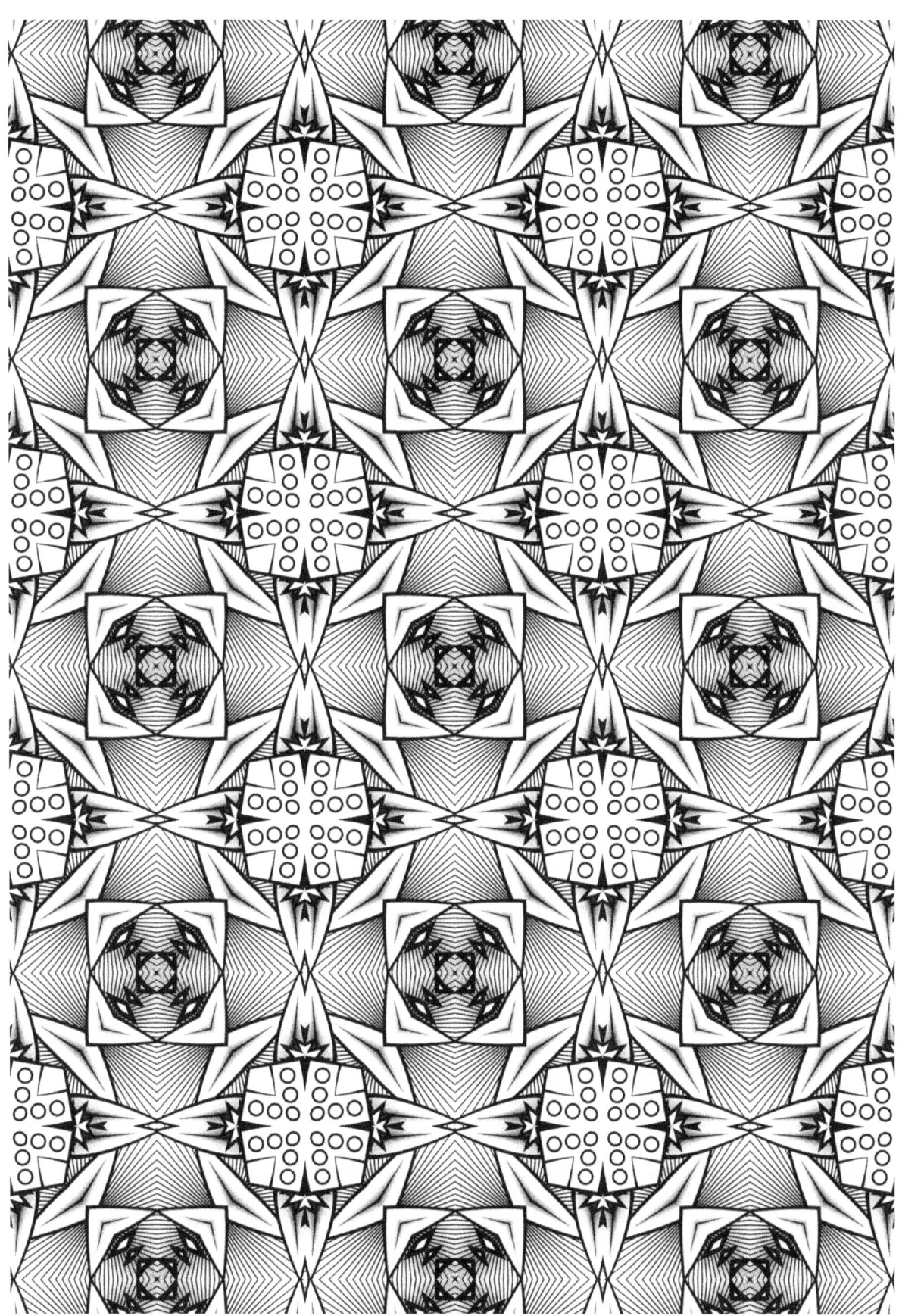

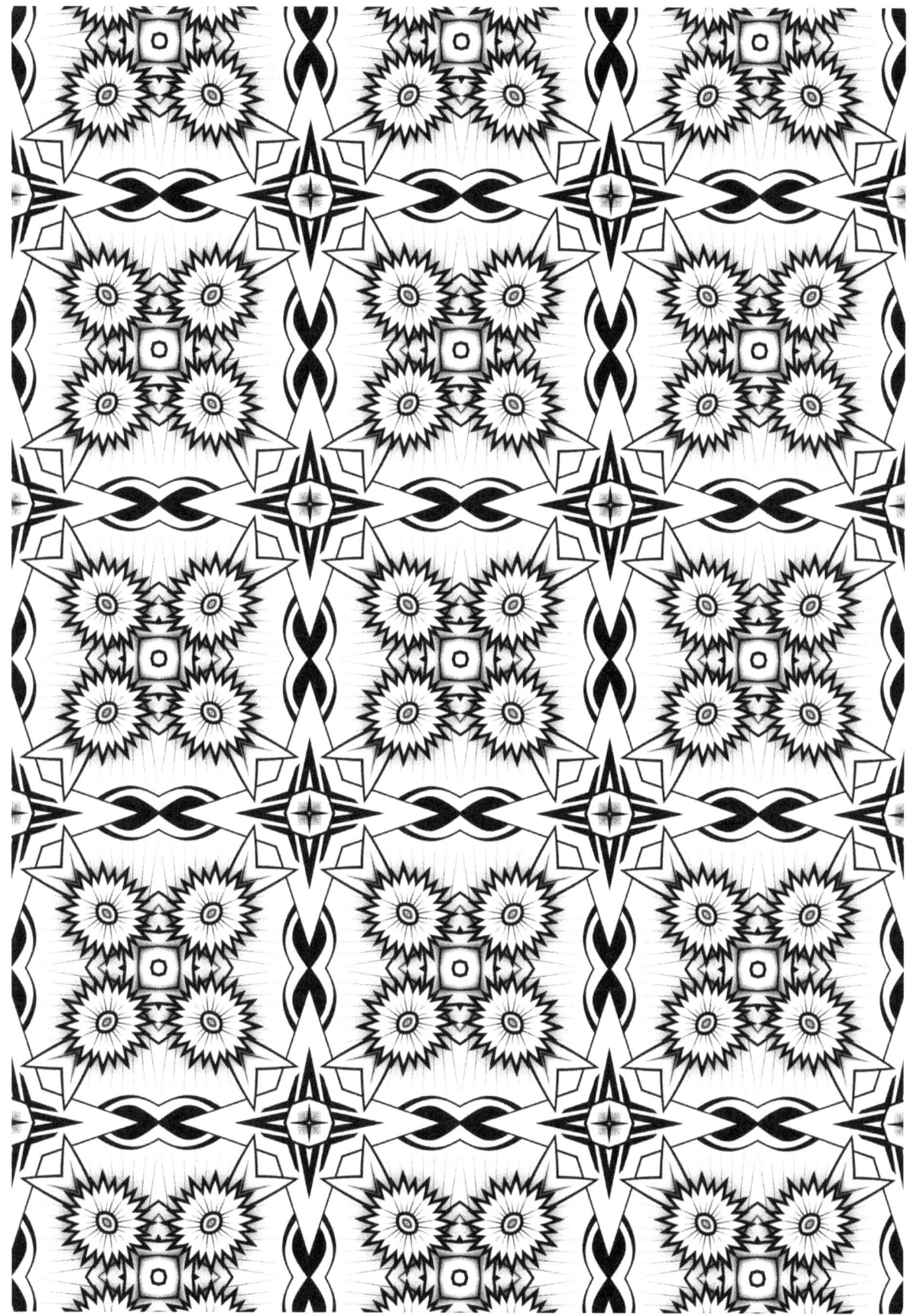

Thank You for your indulgence with Sacred Geometry:Mandalas Vol 1. I hope it's been as much a pleasure for you as it was for me to create it. If you enjoyed this Adult Coloring Book, you're sure to enjoy Sacred Geometry: Mandalas II.

Cordially,

Joseph Leon